MEET JESUS

A book of friendship
for 5-6 year-olds

John Hunt
Publishing Limited

Peter pulled the curtain back and
looked at the night sky.

The stars were shining brightly and the
moon was a beautiful crescent shape.

"Isn't God clever to have made all
this!" says Peter.

God created the whole world.

He made people, children, animals and insects.

He made the mountains, trees and colourful flowers, flowing streams and lovely sunsets.

God must be so wonderful to have created all of this...

Can we *see* Him? Turn to the next
page...

Here is Jesus!

If you look at Jesus you can see God.

Jesus came to live on earth many years ago.

Jesus came to show us how much God loves everyone.

Some bad people killed Jesus.

His friends were very sad.

But after three days, Jesus came back alive.

He then went to meet His friends. They were very surprised and happy to see Him.

Jesus said to them: "I am going away and you won't be able to see me, but don't be afraid because I will always be with you in your heart, for I am ALIVE forever."

Then Jesus went back to His home called
Heaven to be with His Father God.

Jesus loves all children.

He loves you... and always will.

Ask Jesus to be your friend and He will.

Here is a prayer to say:

"Lord Jesus, please be my friend forever.

Amen."

There are sixty minutes in one hour.

That is a lot of minutes in one day.

You could use some of those
minutes to talk to Jesus.

Here is a prayer for you to say:

"Thank you Jesus for everyone who
loves me.
Thank you for being so good to me.
Please bless my family.

Amen."

Sara says "hello" to Jesus every morning.

You can say it, too, when you wake up.

If you ask Jesus, He will help you through the day.

Sarah has just started school. She knows that Jesus will help her to be happy and kind to everyone.

Jesus will help YOU at school.

Peter is on his way to the dentist. He won't be frightened because he knows that Jesus is looking after him.

James is helping Mrs Smith, an elderly lady, by carrying her shopping bag.

Jesus is very pleased with James!

Here is a prayer for you:
"Lord Jesus, show me each day how I can help my family and everybody I know. Thank you.

Amen."

Peter is helping his mum with making a cake. What fun! His mum is very happy that he is helping her.

Perhaps you could help your mum or dad around the home.

That would please Jesus very much.

Read exciting stories about Jesus in the Bible... perhaps with someone helping you.

Read about Jesus helping blind people to see, or helping a man to walk again.

Only Jesus could help these people... because He is GOD!

Poor James has fallen over and
hurt himself.

Sarah and Peter comfort him and put a
plaster on his knee.

One day Sarah would like to be a nurse
and Peter a doctor.

Here is a prayer for you:

"Dear Lord Jesus, when I grow up, help
me to find a job that makes
You happy.

If it makes You happy, I know that I will
be happy too.

Amen."

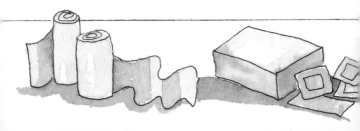

Uncle John is in hospital.

He is feeling much better now because
Peter has been praying for him.

Here is a prayer for you:

"Lord Jesus please help...

> people who are sad or
>
> alone, or
>
> frightened, or
>
> who have no food, or
>
> who have no home.

Dear Jesus, please use my
prayer to make them
happy.

You know what's best
for them.

Amen."

Do you enjoy eating your food?

Sarah and James do. They are going to eat a pizza.

Both of them want to thank Jesus for the meal.

It makes Jesus happy when you do this.

Here is a prayer for you: "Thank You Jesus for all the food You provide for us.

Amen."

Try to talk to Jesus every day.

There are two more prayers over the next page for you.

Morning

Lord Jesus, thank You for this new day.

Help me to remember You with me.

Show me those who are sad ... so that I can give them a smile or be kind to them.

Help me to be kind to everybody ...
   at home
   at school
   when playing with my friends.

Thank You, Lord Jesus.

Evening

Dear Lord Jesus, thank You for all that You have done for me today.

Thank You for keeping me safe.

I'm sorry for the times I have made you sad.

Thank You for loving me so much.

Please look after me tonight ... and for ever.
Thank You, Lord Jesus.